Disclaimer

ZELENE BAKER is the author.

INTRODUCTION

You can tell what kind of building it will be by looking at the foundation.

To be able to support the building, every man who plans to create an upstairs introduces pillars and iron rods of varying diameters. It comes down to relationships and marriage in the same way. First and first, any marriage must be based on Jesus, who is the rock-solid foundation, for it to succeed.

You'll discover once more that the kind of sand or gravel you use for your foundation says volumes about the size of the building. Some use gravel, chippings, and even better, some utilize rocks. And Jesus is the rock that ensures that any marriage has a solid and fruitful basis.

When a building's foundation is solid, no matter how harsh the weather or how many paths it may encounter, it will never experience a crack or collapse.

Jesus narrates the tale of two men who went out to construct in Luke 6:47–48. One rapidly completed their construction on the sand while the second dug down further and constructed their home on the rock. The one on the sand was destroyed by the water, but the one on the rock endured the storm and survived.

Every marriage that must stand should and must be built on the rock that is Christ.

CHAPTER 1

DISCOVERING JESUS: THE TRUE FOUNDATION TO GODLY MARRIAGE

Is your marriage solid or built on shaky ground?

Based on this question, it's necessary that before any relationship or marital home is built, we need to discover that every house must have a foundation, and it is this that makes the house stand solid.

In a Christian marriage, Jesus is that solid and true foundation that should be sought after and discovered.

Being married is a wonderful phase of life because it unites two souls and two journeys under covenants with God. Additionally, it represents Christ's love for His church in a tangible way who is the true foundation. Two people decide to pursue this lifelong commitment after spending the time to get to know, comprehend, and pray for wisdom and direction.

Why then is something so unique and frequently well-planned so challenging? In the end, sin, which creeps into every setting, is the biggest issue with marriage. Even if the individuals involved are redeemed, this union is not between two saints but rather between two sinners who, while they may be saved by grace, nonetheless require the Holy Spirit and God's mercy daily.

The greatest approach to make a marriage stronger from the start and to mend it after it has been harmed is to construct it on the firm Rock of Jesus Christ rather than tossing it onto the destructive rocky shore of life.

Just like in life in general, there will always be storms, difficulties, and difficulties, and all we can do is be ready for them. How? focusing on Jesus. According to John 2, when the wine ran out, the people turned to Jesus for help because he had been invited to their wedding. Through him, they were able to find a solution.

I'm praying for you, sir and ma, that every prayer and request you make to Jesus throughout this marriage would be quickly granted in the name of Jesus.

WORK IN ACCORD.

The agreement is the cornerstone of marriage and keeps it strong.

Therefore, a man must forsake his parents and cleave to his wife, and the two of them must become one, according to Gen 2:24 and Mk 10:7-9. Understandably, long-married couples start to resemble one another when you see them. They are identical in every way.

Two cannot walk together unless they agree, according to Amos 3:3.

According to Matthew 18:19, anything that two of you agree on will be carried out for you.

The agreement is simply being together, constantly doing everything together.

APPRECIATE THE HIERARCHY IN WEDDINGS.

According to 1 Corinthians 2:3, the man is the head of every woman and Christ is the head of every man. This teaches us that whatever a man does, he should report it to Christ, who is his head. Your husband is your head of household, not your friends or your parents, or even your mom. The phrase "I'll tell Daddy for you, I'll tell

Mommy for you" is used by kids. Unfortunately, children cannot get married. Therefore, mother, I'm asking the Lord once more to grant you the grace to mature quickly as you enter this marriage in Jesus' name.

LOVE AND SUBMISSION ARE REQUIRED

Ephesians 5:22 says that wives should submit to their husbands as they would the Lord.

Paul writes in Ephesians 5:24, "Husbands, love your wives as Christ loved the church and gave himself up for it.

SEPARATION AFTER MARRIAGE

Marriage means saying goodbye to some long-time pals who stay up late and to idle friends who drop by to gossip about what their husbands did, can, and can't do.

The separation from parents is the most significant thing. It's time for mommy and daddy to go away and leave the kids alone. Give them the freedom to make errors and learn from them.

Therefore, according to Genesis 2:24, a man must renounce both his mother and father in favor of his bride.

What God has joined together, let no man rip asunder (Mark 10:7-9). Let them make their errors so they can learn.

SELDOM FORGET THE LAST WEDDING.

Every marriage that has ever existed is but a kind of union that will one day exist. It is a union that will unite all believers in Christ, both living and dead, in marriage to the rock-solid Christ.

Any person who skips this wedding will go to hell. It is referred to as the Lamb's marriage feast. Blessed are those who are invited to the marriage feast of the Lamb, according to Rev. 19:9. 1 According to John 3:3 and Thess. 4:16–17, the only requirement for this marriage is that the male is born again. Unless a man is born again.

Chapter 2

FOUNDATIONAL PILLARS FOR MARRIAGE

Marriage is a wonderful partnership in which two people declare to one another, "This is who I am; please accept and love me for the rest of my life. True, being married does not guarantee happiness, and the institution of marriage in America is in peril. Here are some Christian perspectives regarding the ideal of what a Christian marriage could or could be.

"Haven't you read that in the beginning, the Creator Made them male and female,' and said, 'For this reason, a man will leave his father and mother and be wedded to his wife, and the two will become one flesh? Jesus stated the sacredness of Christian marriage. As a result, they are no longer two, but one. Let no man then divide what God has put together.``

As a young guy, I worked as a laborer in construction. The company specialized in unique homes constructed around a lake. One of these concepts was particularly intriguing. The owner had bought a piece of land that was just two sides of a ravine that went to the lake. To build a house there, dirt and rock had to be brought in and deposited into the ravine until it was full. The following compression by large pieces of machinery, piers, or pillars had to be dug into the ground until they reached bedrock. The house, which was quite huge, was erected atop such underground pillars.

Marriage is a house that will be washed away unless it is built on some really strong pillars. I've identified pillars that can help a marriage succeed. Each of these foundational pillars of marriage must be strengthened for it to stand. They are fundamental.

Working on these things with your spouse is essential for a healthy marriage, but bear in mind that all marriages are works in progress. They are all flawed in some way.

LOVE

For us, 1 Corinthians defines love. Love is patient and gentle. It is neither envious, boastful, nor self-assured. It is not harsh, self-seeking, or quickly irritated, and it keeps no record of wrongs. Love does not take pleasure in wickedness, but rather rejoices in the truth. It always guards, always believes, always hopes, and always perseveres.

In Ephesians, 5:25 Paul describes love to wives as being about giving rather than feeling.

Love, as opposed to "being in love," is more than just an emotion. It is a deep oneness maintained by the will and purposefully reinforced by habit; enhanced by (in Christian marriages) the grace that both partners ask and receive from God. They can love each other even if they don't like each other, just as you may love yourself even if you don't like yourself. They can keep this love even when they could easily be "in love" with someone else if they let themselves. "Being in love" drove them to promise faithfulness first, and this quieter love allows them to keep the promise.

The engine of marriage is powered by love; falling in love was the spark that ignited it.
When asked, "Do you love your spouse? Most individuals will examine the topic from the standpoint of being "in love. In other words, people respond to whether or not they are now in love. "Do you love your spouse? is a more action-oriented question. When questioned, "Do you love your spouse? The answer should be based on one's conduct toward his or her spouse. If the answer is "yes, I love my husband/wife," one should

follow it up with "I am devoting myself to him/her.

TRUST

Without trust, it is impossible to build and preserve a good marriage. It is critical to have faith in one another.

There are three main levels of marital trust. Each of these levels is given weighted importance.

The first level is that of faithfulness.

A married person must have faith in his or her spouse to stay faithful to the marriage. God put such value on this aspect of marital trust that He included it as one of the Ten Commandments.

The honesty level is the second level of trust.
A husband or wife should be able to trust his or her partner to be truthful. A partner must be open and honest about who they are, how they feel and think, and their accomplishments and failings. There should be no concealment from one another. They must be able to rely on one another, to tell the truth.

Now, if a spouse lies about something, it does not destroy the foundation of the marriage trust, but it does harm the relationship. One important question to consider is why one's partner lied. The answer to that question is critical to repairing the wound of shattered trust. If a wife, for example, fails to tell her husband that she received a ticket because she is scared he would be furious, and if he has a history of being angry over such things, then both of them must concentrate on healing that wound. She must repair her credibility with him by being honest, and he must make it safe for her to tell the truth by not punishing her with his rage.

The third level of trust is concerned with actions.

In general, a husband or wife wants to believe that his or her spouse will act in specific ways toward him or her. One wants to trust the other to meet needs, to treat him or her with respect, to be patient, and to take him or her into account in daily activities.

The levels of trust are categorized as one, two, or three for the following reasons. A husband who violates his wife's confidence on the first level damages significantly more than he does on the third level. In contrast, if a husband forgets to call his wife to let her know he will be late, it will not have the same devastating effect as cheating. It may have shattered her trust and harmed the relationship, but it did not destroy it and requires less effort to repair.

RESPECT

Respect is how someone treats something they value. When something is highly regarded, it is treated with honor and decency. It is not mistreated or discarded. "How much do I value my spouse? " is a good question to ask.

Marriage partners feel undervalued when they are not treated with respect. This devaluing erodes the pillar and breeds hostility toward one another. According to 1 Peter 2:17, "show suitable respect to everyone.

What must be recognized is that men and women experience respect in various ways. When a man can figure something out and achieve a goal or target, he often feels valued. A woman feels appreciated when she has someone to whom she can talk and be understood.

If it is true that one respects what one values, then it is reasonable to expect a husband and wife to respect one another. The issue is that the way a man displays respect for someone he appreciates is by assisting in the resolution of difficulties and providing solutions. A woman demonstrates her regard for someone

she values by conversing with him or
her.

The goal is to first choose to value
one's partner, and then learn how to
respect him or her in a way that he or
she will understand and enjoy.
If a husband values his wife and she
comes to him with a problem, he
should reconsider his first instinct,
which is to come up with a solution.
He should consider the possibility
that she is not looking for a solution.
She is showing him respect by talking
to him and sharing her feelings.
Coming up with a solution may cause
her to become irritated or upset since
she simply wants to connect, not

solve her problem. When this occurs, the husband may become disappointed or upset because he believes she believes his answer is inadequate.

When her husband achieves something, a wife who values him will express her appreciation. She will strive to grasp his proclivity to "fix" problems and propose solutions.

This is how both men and women are wired. God may have designed humans in this manner to keep boredom at bay. A guy and a woman spend their entire lives trying to figure each other out. Many jokes have been created about men's inability to understand women. Women, on the other hand, have a tough time comprehending men. In all seriousness, the pillar of value for one another means that husbands and wives hold each other in such high regard that they are willing to forsake natural ways of displaying respect to learn how to show respect in ways that their spouse will understand.

UNDERSTANDING

After a mistake, a man wrote to his wife, "Dearest, If I say anything that can be interpreted two ways and one of those ways makes you sad or furious, I meant it the other way.

" You must do the following: speak the truth to one another and deliver true and sound judgment..." Zechariah 8:16.

Understanding one another is a fundamental component of attending school. A husband's job is to become his wife's student. The role of a wife is to become a student of her husband.

A spouse might inquire about the following:
How well do I know my husband?
Do I know what he/she likes to eat?
Do I understand what makes him/her happy? Sad? Frustrated? Angry?

Is it possible for me to predict how he or she would react in various situations?

What is his/her way of thinking and communicating?

Why does he/she feel the way he/she does?

Understanding one's partner is essential for ensuring that one can show respect, communicate well, and be what the other person requires.

There are numerous books and seminars available that address the problem of attempting to understand one's spouse. They all share the notion that a husband may learn about his wife and a wife can learn about her spouse. The idea is to figure out what one's partner understands as love and do that, even if one's natural impulse is to do what makes oneself feel loved.

The bottom line is that for a wonderful marriage to thrive, a husband must become a student of his wife and a lady must become a student of her husband.

FAITH

Faith is the realization that there is something bigger than oneself. It's the prospect of something better. It represents the archetype, the concept of beauty. God has these ideals in mind. Someone sees something and thinks it's beautiful, but what exactly is beauty? God created beauty as a template for all things beautiful.

There is a marriage archetype. It is a concept created by God. Hope grows when one believes in God and the prospect of a good marriage. It is worthwhile to strive for the ideal. It is an unattainable aim, but one that should be held as a lifetime standard. In this writer's humble opinion, two persons of faith who have before them the ideal of marriage as God intended will find the journey of marriage to be the most gratifying of all earthly relationships.

COMMUNICATION

You cannot have a happy marriage if you do not communicate effectively with your partner. This does not only imply that you are conversing with one another, but that you are conversing about important issues.

In some cases, couples simply communicate about what needs to be done, such as chores, the requirements of their children, and their day. You and your spouse should be able to talk about anything, and they should be able to talk about anything with you.

If you don't feel heard or need help fixing a problem in your life, this includes your hopes and dreams.

When you know you can always talk to your partner about anything, and they will listen to you and provide constructive criticism when you need it, it may give you a lot of strength in your marriage.

HONESTY

Honesty is one of the cornerstones of a good marriage because if you are dishonest, your marriage will most likely fail.

You must always be honest with your partner, in both minor and major details. Remember that you chose your spouse for a purpose, and they may surprise you, even if you give them bad news or information.

Instead of lying to them, you owe them the opportunity to comprehend what you have to say.

Another component of honesty that is vital when it comes to marriage pillars is being honest about how you feel and what you require. Sincerity and communication are essential components of any marriage. Keep in mind that you must always be honest in your communication.

Chapter 3

THE PLIGHTS AND ORDEALS OF MARRIAGE

Each partnership experiences its highs and lows. Similar to this, marriage, no matter how happy it is, undoubtedly has its problems.

Nobody intentionally works to ruin their marriage. Everybody wants successful, fulfilling marriages. However, many earnest Christian couples stray into several hazards that harm or occasionally end their relationships because we live in an evil world that silently influences us more than we know. Even though no marriage is flawless, believers' marriages will be strong if they reject the ways of the world and use the guidance of God's Word in their unions.

Remember that God's glory, not our satisfaction, is the primary objective of marriage. Our marriages serve as a reflection of Christ and the church, His bride (Eph. 5:32). We are to show the steadfast, holy love that Christ has for His church to the world (and even to the angelic hosts, Eph. 3:10!). Furthermore, as John Piper frequently notes, "God is most glorified in us when we are most satisfied in Him.

Therefore, the goal of every Christian marriage must be to glorify God.

Paul issues the following broad instructions in the sentence just before he issues direct commands to wives and husbands (Eph. 5:15–17): Because the days are wicked, "be cautious how you move, not as fools but as wise men, making the most of your time. So, instead of acting foolishly, comprehend what the Lord's will is. Instead of going into detail about these verses (for that, read my talk, "Walking Wisely," in the Ephesians series), I'm going to make a general application to marriage:

We live in a period of adversity, so protect your marriage by avoiding worldly perils and using God's knowledge. If you are not attentive, numerous threats in this terrible world will ruin your marriage.

These threats vary in their potential for death. The harm is increased if you fall into more than one. The following "dirty dozen" external threats to your marriage include:

Communication problems

One of the most common causes of marital issues is poor communication. It might appear in a variety of ways. Paul states in Ephesians 4:15 that we must "grow up into Him who is the head, even Christ," by speaking the truth in love. Christ is to be the head and the Lord of all our communication. Ask yourself, "Will my words be pleasant to the Lord Jesus Christ? before you speak. And, "Are my statements sincere and kind, intended to strengthen my relationship with Christ? It may be true to criticize your partner because "that's just how I feel," but it is not loving. Although it may seem loving to be untruthful about how you feel or to stay silent to avoid conflict, doing so will cause the relationship to drift apart over time. Time constraints prevent me from saying more, but the church website contains a one-page guide titled "Some Biblical Principles for Communication.

Anger and threatening language: Sinful rage always harms relationships. But everyone should be quick to hear, slow to speak, and slow to get angry since human wrath does not bring about the righteousness of God, James 1:19–20 advises. Let only words that are appropriate for edifying in light of the situation come out of your lips, Paul instructs (Eph. 4:29), Ephesians 4:31 continues, "Let every bitterness and wrath and anger and clamor [yelling] and slander and all malice be taken away from you.

According to Proverbs 15:1, "A soft reply turns away wrath, while a severe declaration kindles anger.

All of those scriptures make the supposition that if you choose to follow God, you will be able to restrain your wrath. Therefore, the justification "I just have a short fuse" won't do! The Lord inquires of Cain in the earliest recorded instance of "counseling" (Gen. 4:6), "Why are you angry? The Lord wasn't considering the solution to that query! He wished for Cain to reflect on the source of his rage in his heart. Selfishness is the primary cause of all rage: "I wanted my way and I didn't get my way! When we become enraged, we are not acknowledging God's sovereignty, which is in charge of all the challenging and upsetting circumstances that enter our life. Couples who are married often use rage as a means of intimidation and control. However, it always drives a wedge between partners and is disastrous!

Bitterness and a refusal to forgive:
Paul adds (Eph. 4:32) "Be kind to one another, tenderhearted, forgiving each other, just as God in Christ also has forgiven you" after directing (Eph. 4:31) "Let all bitterness and wrath and anger and clamor [yelling] and slander be put away from you, along

with all malice. Forgiveness is the cure for anger and resentment. Married couples will inevitably wrong each other over time. If they do not address those wrongs in God's way, resentment and bitterness gradually become a wall between them.

Thus, it's crucial to maintain brief correspondence with your partner. Don't remark, "I'm sorry I yelled at you, but your persistence makes me angry," if you lost your cool and yelled at her. This would be blaming her for your sin. Never even apologize for yelling at you. She might be regretful and that might be the case. While expressing regret does not absolve you of guilt for your sin, it does express how you are feeling. Saying, "God has convinced me of my sinful rage and I've requested His forgiveness" is the correct response to your transgression. I'll make an effort to fight that sin. I'm requesting your forgiveness. As Christians, we are obligated to pardon those who beg for our pardon (Matt. 6:14-15; 18:21-35). Saying "I forgive you" will help to mend the connection.

Because Jesus indicated that all immorality starts in the heart, I want to underline that sexual immorality starts on the mental level (Mark 7:21-

23; Matt. 5:27-28). So, guys, if you're looking at pornography or covertly lusting after women other than your wife, you're ruining your marriage. You're heading down a path that ends in bodily immorality. Furthermore, Jesus warned that if you don't take drastic measures to eliminate mental lust from your life—like plucking out your eye or chopping off your hand—you'll end up in hell (Matt. 5:29–30)! Jesus expressed it strongly; I wouldn't have.

Although Christian academics have different interpretations, I believe that God authorizes divorce in circumstances of physical sexual immorality outside of marriage (Matthew 5:31–32; 19:3–9). God's best, however, is always reconciliation in marriages. God frequently accuses His people Israel of spiritual adultery against Him in the Old Testament. But He continually extends an invitation to turn from their sin and come back to Him. He only divorces them after several instances of adultery (Jer. 3:6-10). Since the purpose of marriage is to exalt God, I think that reconciling and repairing a marriage exalts God more than breaking it up. God's best is never quick or simple, but it always takes time.

Drug and alcohol abuse:

I've seen many Christian homes torn apart by these vices. Many contend that drug and alcohol addiction are diseases. That is partially true, but not entirely. Although they are both sins, both types of abuse also have a physical component. When a person becomes addicted to a substance, his body begins to want it, and he frequently resorts to lying, stealing, or worse to obtain it. It is erroneous to argue that using drugs and alcohol is not a sin because doing so absolves the offender of accountability.

However, no one has ever developed a drug or alcohol addiction without deciding to take the first drink or dose. The Bible views intoxication as a sinful act of the flesh and condemns it (Gal. 5:21). Since God is in the business of giving His people victory over sin, admitting that something is sin is the first step to being delivered from it.

Although the Bible permits moderate alcohol consumption, it can nonetheless be risky. You are breaking the law if you use alcohol to deal with your problems or relieve stress because you aren't putting your faith in the Lord for these things. Utilizing drugs or alcohol is a sin that will destroy your marriage.

Selfishness:

There are several ways to be selfish. As I already stated, rage stems from selfishness. A self-centered husband won't consider other viewpoints and is adamant that he is correct. He just considers his wants and his feelings, not his wife's needs or potential feelings. For himself, he will buy whatever he wants, but not for his wife. He won't allow his wife to spend time with her friends because he wants her to be accessible to suit his needs, but he will spend time with his buddies when he feels like it.

Self and the many ways in which it manifests itself are always the true root of marriage failure. That is the root of all problems in all spheres. The greatest disruptive forces in the world are ego and selfishness.

As said by Jesus in Luke 9:23, "If anybody intends to come after Me, he must deny himself, and take up his cross daily and follow Me," we must daily put ourselves to death to follow Him. The second greatest commandment, according to Matthew 22:39, is to love one's neighbor as oneself. My wife is the closest person to me. I have to fight my selfishness every day to love her.

Many Christian couples are competing for authority and power in their marriages rather than working together. It frequently manifests itself in the way they trade scathing remarks or attempt to diminish one another through comedy. They would protest, "We're just joking," if you were to confront them. However, rivalry undermines the truth that we are members of one another and that our goal should be to strengthen one another, whether in marriage or the church (Eph. 5:28-30).

You have a serious issue if your arm is fighting against the rest of your body. The members of your body should work together rather than compete for the benefit of all.

I made it clear to Marla before our wedding that I did not want us to smash cake in each other's faces as a sign of disrespect or to begin competing with one another. I used to tell her in the early years of our marriage that I was on her side and that I only wanted what was best for her if she was upset with me about something. If I did you wrong, I want to make it right. However, we are on the same side. We need to collaborate.

If a significant doctrinal or moral problem is not at stake, you should not try to win a debate or argument. Your goal should be to learn to work together as a couple to bring glory to the Lord.

Not Meeting up in monetary obligations:

I've read that conflicts about finances frequently lead to divorce. Sometimes an extravagant spender may wed a frugal person who won't purchase anything unless it's on sale, can be found at a thrift shop, or is necessary. We have a problem, as the infamous understatement goes, in Houston. Such a pair will have to put forth an extra effort to coexist peacefully. Studying what the Bible teaches about financial stewardship is a good place to start.

If couples are competing instead of working together, the issue will get worse. They start bickering over money: "You got yourself that new motorcycle we couldn't afford, therefore I'm taking my buddies to Hawaii! The marriage is under extreme stress as a result of mounting debt and credit card interest. That strain is not necessary! The answer is to handle your finances following the guidelines found in God's Word. Make a strategy to pay off your debt first, and then live within your means after that.

Time mismanagement:

According to Paul, if we are wise, we will make the most of our time. However, it's simple to become a workaholic and neglect your loved ones. Or, many families end up having too many activities on their plates. Or perhaps a husband and wife are not spending enough time together because they are heading in different directions.

Early in the marriage, it's common for the spouse to devote all of his attention to his profession, putting in the necessary hours to succeed. If I don't do this, I'll get passed over for promotion or even fired," he justifies his long days or numerous business trips. The wife's time is devoted to raising the family's numerous children because of this. If she is working at another job in addition, she scarcely has any free time. The pair drifts apart as a result of their busy schedules.

Meanwhile, the devil brings along a lovely, engaging young woman at work who, unlike the exhausted wife at home, provides the husband with attention and affirmation. Another option is that a man at work supplies a need that the wife's exhausted husband is no longer able to provide if she works. He is patient, compassionate, and willing to hear what she has to say. He exudes such compassion. It's a set-up for marital infidelity, whether with the husband or the wife. It all starts with poor time management, which causes your marriage to suffer in favor of other priorities.

Wrong aims and expectations:
Many couples have unspoken expectations when they get married. Conflict is inevitable if a guy expects his wife to stay at home, take care of the house, and watch the kids while she hopes to have a prosperous profession. A train wreck is in the making if a wife expects her new husband to produce a ton of money so they may advance in society and live the good life, but he expects to live

cheaply and donate the remainder to missions!

The solution is to discuss expectations and mutually decide on biblical marriage goals. It's not a good idea to prioritize career success over marital success. It's not a good objective to live to impress others by acquiring a larger and finer home, a newer and more expensive automobile, or more possessions. Paul cautions in 1 Timothy 6:7–10:

We cannot take anything from the world because we did not contribute anything to it. We will be pleased as long as we have food and shelter. But people who seek wealth fall prey to temptation, a trap, and several harmful and foolish pursuits that lead to men's downfall and destruction. Because the desire for money is the source of all evil, many people have strayed from their religion and suffered greatly as a result.

Jesus said in Matthew 6:33 what our aim should be, not all the things that the pagans seek: But put God's kingdom and righteousness first, and everything else will be added to you. Every couple should discuss and agree upon what that means in terms of time and money management. It is not an eternal conversation. At various stages of marriage, putting God's kingdom and righteousness first will appear different. However, that should always be a couple's main objective.

Worldliness:

Adopting worldly ideals, objectives, and practices instead of those found in God's Word is known as being worldly. Be vigilant because worldliness might sneak into your life while you're not paying attention. "Marriage is to make you happy," the consensus is. You should get a divorce and look for a new partner if your marriage isn't making you happy. Your lifelong marriage is to reflect the bond between Christ and the church, according to God, and to bring Me honor.

The roles of men and women in marriage are up for debate, the globe declares. Whoever does what is fine as long as you both agree on it. The Bible states that wives are to submit to their husbands with respect and that husbands are to lead in love. The entire globe is urging you to defend your rights. The Bible commands us to put the needs and interests of others ahead of our own (Phil. 2:3-8). The consensus is that "having more possessions will make you happier. What good will it do for a man if he obtains the whole world but loses his soul, asked Jesus (Matt. 16:26)? Finally,

Drifting from the Lord:

When I speak at weddings, I frequently make the analogy that God is at the apex of a triangle, and the bride and groom are at the bottom two corners. The pair gets to know each other better as they progress in their relationship with the Lord. Alternatively, if they move oppositely, they will grow further apart. They will become more devoted to one another as they develop the characteristics listed under "love, joy, peace, patience, kindness, goodness, faithfulness, gentleness, and self-control" (Gal. 5:22–23). However, the works of the body, include immorality (Gal. 5:19–21).

Chapter 4

UNDERSTANDING YOUR WIFE AND PROVIDING FOR HER NEEDS

Understanding is essential to having a healthy relationship with your girlfriend; most failed marriages and relationships suffer from a lack of understanding between partners.

Do you think your wife is acting too sentimentally? Do you wish you could understand her occasionally strange behavior? Even though women's brains are structured differently from men's, there are techniques to comprehend your wife and strengthen your relationship with her.

Seven Most Important Things Your Wife Needs

I have counseled and ministered to married couples throughout the years, mostly those who were in crisis, and I have observed some patterns that are quite consistent in each relationship. In reality, couples are not all that dissimilar from one another. To make their marriages the best they can be, most men and women bring certain needs to the relationship. Although we may use different names, the requirements are essentially the same regardless of the marriage. Even though they are based on my findings, many couples seem to find them to be true.

I've also come to understand that identifying needs is the first step in meeting them. Only what we already know is known. We look forward to having a better grasp of one another's needs.

Here are the top seven desires of a wife:

1. Love

Philippians 5:25 As Christ loved the church and gave Himself up for her, husbands, "love your wives as yourself. How did Christ show the church his love? "This is how we know what love is: Jesus Christ laid down his life for us," declares 1 John 3:16.

Do you, as a man, value your wife more than anything else in your life—aside from your relationship with Christ—including your job, your hobbies, your friends, your family, and even the kids? Do your words and, more importantly, your actions match up?

2. Paying heed

Even when the television is on, wives want to know that we value what they have to say and that they are being heard. Even though another woman would be able to understand us better, our wives would choose to speak with us.

Are you men paying attention to what your wife is saying? Do your actions, once more, support this?

3. Security

Wives want their husbands to protect the family from all hazards in society, not only from strange noises at night. They want us to take responsibility for spiritually guiding our family and for teaching our children how to stand strong and defend themselves in a hostile environment.

Men, are you doing all you can to keep your family safe from harm?

4. Security and dedication

The woman wants to know if you intend to stay there indefinitely. Wives frequently see their visibly animated husbands looking at other women. Does she understand that you won't betray her? Will you remain dependable?

Can she trust you, men? Do your actions bolster that self-assurance?

5. Value/Appreciation

Wives desire to be respected both for who they are and for their accomplishments. Wives want to know that we value them beyond what they do to maintain the household. Does she matter more than what she does? Does she still have beauty?

Do you regularly tell her what you like about her, men? Do you truly praise her rather than merely praising what she does?

6. Compassion

Women are referred to in the Bible as "weaker vessels. Of course, this doesn't imply that they are inferior to men, just that they are different. Women will react to situations differently. They might cry more readily, process emotions more slowly, and get tired more quickly. Ladies also desire some romance in their marriages. (For most of us, if our marriages have lasted longer than a week, they already know it won't happen with you.) But we could all be loving, compassionate, and occasionally romantic. We routinely get decent marks around here just by trying.

Do you realize that your wife is not wired the same way you are, men? Are you kind to her and do you let her handle things differently than you? Are you still making an effort to pursue your wife romantically, like you did before you got married?

7. Collaboration

Wives prefer not to navigate life alone. They want their husband to take an active role in parenting, household decision-making, and, occasionally, even choosing paint colors. They don't want to lead two separate lives in the same home; they want someone to do life with them.

THE ESSENTIALS FOR SATISFYING HER NEED

Accept her feelings:
Recognize that God has given your wife's emotions to her as a gift. Do not underestimate them. Validate her sentiments as she uses them to solve problems in her life rather than attempting to suppress them.

Pay attention to what she says:
Tell her that you value her opinion and that you'll hold off on deciding until you've heard it from her entirely. Give her your undivided attention as she speaks, without any interruptions like the television on in the background. Make sure to look her in the eye, nod in agreement as she speaks to show that you are listening, and repeat key points she makes to make sure you understand them.

Never attempt to solve her problems when she discusses them with you:
Be aware that women often verbalize their thoughts to evaluate them. You should be aware that your wife wants

you to support her views when she expresses them rather than try to give her unwelcome advice. As you simply listen to her and guide her along the way, let her try to deal with her worries. Ask her questions that might enable her to come up with a solution on her own. You could inquire, for instance, "What would you desire the outcome of this to be, and why?

Exhibit nonsexual physical love:
Be aware that if a woman's husband solely offers her physical contact that results in sexual intimacy, she may feel used. Nurture your wife by giving her a backrub, a hug, or other affection without anticipating sex in

return. Your wife should become more sexually sensitive when you do make love if you often engage in nonsexual touch.

Speak with her:

Recognize that women spell intimacy T-A-L-K, not sex (S-E-X) like men do (S-E-X). Tell her everything about your life. Without holding anything back from your wife, talk to her about every aspect of your life, including your career and friends.

Pray with and for her:

Inform you how you have been praying for your wife and that you should continue to do so. Pray with her whenever you can, and while you do, trust that God will strengthen your spiritual relationship.

Be aware of her hormonal changes: Recognize that her hormones may influence her moods at various periods throughout the month. Discuss this with your wife, and prepare for the changes so you can handle them when they happen in a kind and sensible way.

Give her the impression that she is your top priority:

Save part of your time and energy for your wife at the end of each day rather than spending it all at work or elsewhere. Plan your day to accommodate your interaction with her.

Be her closest friend and support her female friendships:
Share leisure activities and help her schedule regular outings with her female pals. Be aware that female bonding enhances women's emotional stamina.

Protect your connection:
Keep your emotional bond with her strength to prevent her from being

enticed to satisfy her emotional demands with a different man. Avoid sharing too many personal details with other women, and keep your distance from flirtatious women. Set clear boundaries and reassure your wife that you are only committed to her to avoid being persuaded to have an emotional or physical affair.

Go after romance:
Take the time and make the effort to discover what your wife finds romantic. then engage in such activities frequently.

Give her your undying love and let her know it:

Ask God to help you accept your wife's faults and handle her flaws with kindness. Tell her that you won't ever abandon her.

Always thank her through words and Actions:

Look for opportunities to express your gratitude to her, such as after she completes a task to help you. Let her know that you appreciate all of her efforts.

Chapter 5

A DANGEROUS HUSBANDS FACTORS

Men are from Mars, women are from Venus, goes a classic adage used to explain the behavioral differences between men and women. This quote, attributed to well-known author John Gray, only emphasizes how crucial it is to comprehend each person's unique traits and the behaviors that they share in common. Men have been known to engage in several common vices in marriages, though to varying degrees depending on their exposure.

You might have recently gotten married or been married for a while and are wondering why the man you thought was prim and proper has suddenly developed some terrible habits. Trust me; every man has them, and here are some top negative habits your husband may have that may be driving you crazy.

Dishonesty

This is a poor habit your spouse may have picked up while he was still single, and you may have noticed it while you were courting him because it is frequently apparent. A marriage depends on trust, and if your partner is dishonest, he or she will frequently lie to you about even the most minor matters.

Jealousy

Due to his low self-esteem, does your husband feel a great deal of insecurity in your marriage? As the head of the family and the woman has become the earner, many men nowadays are unable to satisfy their financial obligations. An individual with low self-esteem may get envious as a result of this circumstance.

Intimidating/Coercive

When you find yourself in an intimidating marriage, the proverb that "real men don't intimidate their wives" will be useless to you. Being coercive is a horrible habit, and many women today are suffering through their marriages at the hands of bullies who pass for husbands.

Flirting

True and unconditional love is the foundation of a wonderful marriage, but sadly, many marriages nowadays are arranged for practical reasons, which frequently results in conditional love. If the feelings are not shared, your spouse can find enjoyment in flirting with other women in your place.

Superiority

Some males were conditioned to believe that they were superior to women, and this belief can cause problems in their marriages when they start to assert control over situations that they haven't truly earned. If your husband feels superior to you, he will be patronizing and frequently ask for far more than you can provide because he thinks he is doing you a favor.

Pretense

As many husbands today have perfected the poor habit of treating their wives politely at social gatherings far from what is appropriate at home to create a false picture, indeed, men can also masquerade in marriage. Unfortunately, you find yourself limited to playing the role of the ideal wife of the best husband in town within his scripts.

Loyalty

A man who was raised in a close-knit family is more likely to choose his parents before his wife when it comes to loyalty and dedication. It can be frustrating to live in a marriage that is only second best, and perhaps your husband is the ideal illustration of this awful habit.

Refuses to acknowledge his errors

His ego couldn't handle having to admit he might be mistaken. He is so self-centered that he can only perceive things from his point of view. This indicates that he is always correct and will not take into account your opinion, even if it is supported by evidence.

He greatly undervalues your intelligence while greatly overestimating his own.

His default stance is "I'm right, and you are wrong," for this reason.

Makes every decision by themselves
Your self-centered husband has accepted plans without inquiring about your existing plans.
He wouldn't even consider consulting you because, in your opinion, he has terrible communication skills. He believes that you would blindly comply with anything he decides.

Chapter 6

IDENTITIES OF A DANGEROUS WIFE

A dangerous wife has great negative traits she can be reckoned with. It's a visible character that is not hidden. They are as follows:

1. Ignoring my husband

Being impolite to your husband when you speak to him is the first and most evident evidence that you are a terrible wife. Being disrespectful to your husband when you speak to him is not a good thing. Your husband is your partner in this game of life, and treating him badly could cause you to lose the backing of someone who is supposed to be the cornerstone of your support system.

2. Prohibit the husband from visiting his loved ones

This is something that many wives do, and it is not good. You must keep in mind that your husband has other people in his life than you. He has friends and family, and they ought to be allowed to be a part of his life as well.

Therefore, you are checking off some boxes in the "bad wife" category if you find yourself limiting your husband's time with his friends and telling him he can't see family or that they aren't permitted to visit.

3. Being disrespectful in public or in front of children

Your kids shouldn't witness you fighting since it will diminish their respect for you and their belief in your parental authority. You should be aware that if you insult your husband in front of your children by mocking or disparaging him, it's likely that your kids will do the same.

Another indication that you're a lousy wife is when you disrespect your husband outside by hanging your dirty laundry in the open. This is problematic since it makes him look less impressive to others and is likely to hurt his self-esteem.

4. Overreacting

Do you feel the desire to exert total control over your husband's life? This is bad and might indicate more serious psychological problems. Your husband shouldn't be treated as a slave because he is an independent human being.

5. Would rather spend less time with her husband

Many relationship norms still hold since marriage is just a relationship on steroids. You must spend time together, which is one very important requirement. If you frequently find yourself doing things alone, meeting up with friends frequently, or even spending most of your time with your children instead of your spouse, this is negative and has to change since your husband deserves to spend time with his wife as well.

6. Put a strain on your finances.

A partner's role in a relationship is to push it forward, and a big part of this has to do with money. A wife who drags the marriage down by making poor financial decisions that strain the union is terrible. For instance, you are most definitely in the "bad wife zone" if you continue to accrue debt or make ridiculously expensive requests for one reason or another despite knowing the family cannot afford them.

7. Fight when you could talk
In a marriage, conflict is commonplace.

You two will undoubtedly step on each other's toes and need to sort things out. It's not good if you realize that, rather than conversing with your husband, you usually start a fight.

Since most sides get defensive and resentful during disagreements, they rarely resolve issues. Instead of pushing the discussion to an argument, try to keep it civil.

8. Too attached.

Regardless of how much you or your husband love one another, you must give him room to operate independently. You shouldn't try to follow him at all times, even when he wants to hang out with his buddies. While doing this occasionally is okay and demonstrates your love for your husband, everything should be done in proportion.

And even if he doesn't mind, you still need to enforce this rule because being overly dependent on someone else is not regarded as healthy.

9. A lack of ambition and ambitions

As we previously stated, partners should work to advance the partnership. A woman without goals and aspirations cannot make a significant contribution to the marriage and is consequently a poor wife and partner.

A homemaker can have ambitions and aspirations based on her responsibilities. You should always strive to do things better. In any way you can, you should try to advance your marriage, as doing so would make you a good wife.

10. Are dishonest

This is an obvious choice. You are most definitely a horrible wife if you are cheating on your spouse by engaging in extracurricular "activities" without his consent. You committed your husband when you got married, and anything that goes against that is unquestionably bad.

11. Ignore the husband's feelings

Your husband experiences a lot of difficulties, just like you, which could depress him. In these situations, a horrible wife wouldn't recognize this and would instead reprimand him and make him feel less of a man by telling him to "be a man" and "suck it up.

When your husband offers an opinion about something and you disregard it and still go with it despite having said you wouldn't, that is another instance in which you may be disregarding your husband's sentiments.

12. Keep your husband in the dark and violate his trust.

You shouldn't withhold information about events that occur while you are his wife or material matters that occurred before the marriage but may have an impact on your husband.

Bad wives would engage in illicit behavior, including flirting with other women, seeing acquaintances they had promised not to, and hiding their financial information. When secrets are revealed, trust is betrayed, and no matter how well things go from that point on, nothing will ever be the same.

13. Tell your hubby a lie

In some ways, lying to your husband is worse than harboring secrets since, unlike the former, when you lie to him, you are intentionally leading him astray.

Your husband needs the truth about whatever it is you are doing since you are a team, and surprise parties don't count. This will allow you to make decisions together like the team you are.

CHAPTER 7

BIBLICAL KEYS FOR MARITAL EXCELLENCE

These are the tragedies associated with divorce: resentful ex-spouses, unfulfilled promises, and perplexed kids. Don't let your family experience this!

The Bible provides tried-and-true advice to help your marriage last, regardless of whether it is going well or through difficult times—or even if you are not yet married but are thinking about getting married. God, who created and established marriage, is giving us counsel! Give Him a chance if you've tried everything else first.

Here are a few Biblical keys that will guarantee your marital bliss and make your home or relationship heaven on earth.

Create your private residence

A guy must separate from his parents and marry his wife for them to become one flesh (Genesis 2:24).

A married couple should leave their parents' homes and create their own according to God's principles, even if this means living in a small apartment because of their financial situation. If someone disagrees, a husband and wife should determine this collectively and firmly. The quality of many marriages would increase if this idea was rigorously applied.

Keep up the relationship

Above all, love one another ardently because "love will hide a multitude of sins" (1 Peter 4:8).

Her husband gives her admiration (Proverbs 31:28).

When a woman is married, she is concerned with doing her husband's will (1 Corinthians 7:34).

Be nice and affectionate to one another, giving preference to one another out of respect (Romans 12:10).

Keep up with or renew your courting after you get married

Successful unions must be cultivated; they do not just happen. Don't take one another for granted; else, the boredom that results could ruin your relationship. By communicating your love for one another, you can keep it from fading and causing you to drift away. You don't find love and happiness by looking for them for yourself, but by offering them to others.

Spend as much time as you can together doing stuff. Learn to give each other a cheery greeting. Unwind, chat, do sightseeing, and share food. Don't ignore the small gestures of courtesy, support, and affection. Send each other a present or a favor as a surprise. Attempt to "out-love" one another. Do not attempt to extract more from your marriage than you have invested.

"The worst enemy of marriage is a lack of affection."

Keep in mind that God made your marriage possible
For this reason, a guy must separate from his parents and wed his bride. They are now one flesh rather than two. Therefore, do not let man divide what God has joined together (Matthew 19:5, 6).

Has love all but vanished from your house?

Remember that God Himself joined you together in marriage, and He desires that you stay together and be happy, despite the devil's attempts to tear your marriage apart by persuading you to give up. If you follow His heavenly instructions, He will bring joy and love into your lives. All things are possible with God (Matthew 19:26).

Don't give up. If you ask and allow the Holy Spirit, He can change your heart and the heart of your spouse.

Be careful what you think

"He is what he thinks in his heart" (Proverbs 23:7).

"You shall not desire the wife of your neighbor" (Exodus 20:17).
Keep your heart with all diligence because troubles in life arise from it (Proverbs 4:23).

"Meditate on whatever things are true, noble, just, pure, beautiful, and of good repute" (Philippians 4:8).

Thinking the incorrect way might seriously damage your marriage. The devil will entice you with ideas like "We can always divorce if necessary," "She doesn't understand me," "I can't take much more of this," "I'll go home to mom," or "He smiled at that woman.

This way of thinking is risky because your actions are ultimately determined by your thoughts. Avoid everything that suggests being unfaithful from what is spoken, written, heard, or seen, as well as from those who imply it. Uncontrolled thoughts are like a car in neutral on a steep hill; the outcome could be a catastrophe.

Never argue with one another before night

"Do not let your rage wane as the sun sets" (Ephesians 4:26).

Declare your transgressions to one another (James 5:16).

Forgetting what has passed in the past (Philippians 3:13).

"Be kind and compassionate to one another, forgiving one another just as God, through Christ, has forgiven you" (Ephesians 4:32).

It might be risky to harbor resentment for slight or major wrongs. Even little issues, if not resolved right away, can negatively impact your outlook on life by solidifying your mind as convictions. God commanded us to let our wrath calm before going to bed because of this. Be willing to apologize and extend forgiveness. Because you and your partner are on the same team and understand that nobody is perfect, be generous enough to acknowledge when you make a mistake. Making up is also a really enjoyable process that has the remarkable ability to bring married couples closer together. God advises it! It works!

Maintain Christ as the focal point of your home

They who build the house toil in vain unless the Lord erects it. (Psalm 127:1)

Recognize Him in all your deeds, and He will guide your steps (Proverbs 3:6).

"And through Christ Jesus, the peace of God, which transcends all understanding, will guard your hearts and minds" (Philippians 4:7).

This is the most important concept since it makes others possible. Instead of using diplomacy, strategy, or our efforts to solve issues, the key to domestic happiness lies in a union with Christ. Hearts brimming with Christ's love won't be separated for very long. The likelihood of a marriage succeeding is higher when Christ is present in the family. Jesus has the power to restore love and happiness while washing away bitterness and disappointment.

Join in prayer

"Watch and pray to avoid falling prey to temptation. The flesh is weak, even while the spirit is willing (Matthew 26:41).

Pray for each other (James 5:16).

If any of you lack understanding, let that person ask of God, for He is a generous Giver (James 1:5).

Pray together as a group! This is a beautiful hobby that will go far in ensuring the success of your marriage. Pray to God on your knees for genuine love for one another, forgiveness, strength, knowledge, and solutions to challenges. God will respond. While God won't be able to correct every problem right away, He will have more power to influence your thoughts and behavior.

Recognize that divorcing is not the solution

"Let not man put asunder what God has placed together" (Matthew 19:6). According to the law, a wife must support her husband for as long as he is alive (Romans 7:2).

Marriage relationships are supposed to be unbreakable, according to the Bible. Only in instances of infidelity is divorce permitted. Even so, it is not required. Even in cases of infidelity, forgiveness is always preferable to divorce.

God created the first marriage in Eden with the intention of it lasting forever. Therefore, the promises made during a marriage ceremony are among the most serious and legally binding. But keep in mind that God intended marriage to enrich our lives and fulfill all of our wants.

Maintaining divorce-related ideas might seriously harm your marriage. Divorce is nearly never a solution to a problem; instead, it almost always causes new ones, such as financial difficulties, heartbroken children, etc.

Keep in mind that nagging and criticism erode affection

Love your wife and don't harbor resentment toward them, husbands (Colossians 3:19).

"An argumentative woman is like a constant drip on a very rainy day" (Proverbs 27:15).

Why do you consider the plank (complete board) in your eye but not the speck (splinter) in your brother's eye? (3: Matthew).

"Love does not parade itself; love does not envy; love endures long and is compassionate" (1 Corinthians 13:4).

Quit picking on, nagging, and criticizing your partner

Even if your partner has many shortcomings, you shouldn't criticize them. Expecting perfection will make you and your spouse resentful. Look over flaws and for the positives. Never attempt to change, manage, or persuade your partner—you will sabotage love. People can only be changed by God. A good sense of humor, a positive outlook, kindness, patience, and affection will solve a lot of your marital issues. The excellent will probably take care of itself if you focus on making your partner happy rather than on the good. Not finding the ideal partner, but being that partner is the key to a happy marriage.

Respect each other's rights and privacies

"Love suffers long and is gentle; … Love does not envy … does not behave rudely, does not seek its own [in selfishness] … does not rejoice in iniquity … believes all things, hopes all things, endures all things" (1 Corinthians 13:4–7).

"Be cordially sympathetic to one another with brotherly love, in honor giving preference to one another" (Romans 12:10).

Each couple has a God-given right to some personal privacies

Do not interfere with each other's wallets or purses, personal email, and other private property without giving permission. The right to privacy and quietude when preoccupied should be honored. Marriage partners do not own each other and should never try to compel personality changes. Only God can accomplish such transformations. Confidence and confidence in one another are crucial for happiness, so don't check up on each other constantly. Spend less time attempting to "figure out" your spouse and more time trying to delight her or him. This works wonders.

Keep the family circle closed firmly

"You shall not commit adultery" (Exodus 20:14).

"… She does him good and not evil all the days of her life" (Proverbs 31:11, 12).

"The Lord has been a witness between you and the wife of your childhood, with whom you have acted treacherously" (Malachi 2:14).

Remove your sight from the strange woman

… Do not yearn after her beauty in your heart, nor let her captivate you with her eyelids. Can a guy take fire to his bosom, and his clothes not be burned? … So is he who goes into his neighbor's wife; whoever touches her shall not be innocent" (Proverbs 6:24, 25, 27, 29).

Private family concerns should never be communicated with anybody outside your home—not even your parents

A person outside the marriage to sympathize with or listen to concerns might be used by the devil to estrange the hearts of a husband and wife. Solve your private home problems confidentially. Avoid third parties, unless based on a minister or a marriage counselor, should take part in healing the wound. Always be truthful with each other, and never harbor secrets. Avoid delivering jokes at the expense of your spouse's feelings, and strongly defend each other. God, who knows our thoughts, body, and affections, says, "You shall not commit adultery" (Exodus 20:14). If flirtations have already begun, break them up immediately—or shadows could settle over your life that cannot be readily lifted.

Be tidy, humble, orderly, and dutiful

"In like manner likewise, that the women adorn themselves in modest apparel" (1 Timothy 2:9).

"She … happily works with her hands. … She also awakens while it is night, and provides meals for her home. … She looks over the ways of her home and does not eat the bread of idleness" (Proverbs 31:13, 15, 27).
"Be clean" (Isaiah 52:11).
"Let all things be done tastefully and in order" (1 Corinthians 14:40).
"Do not become sluggish [lazy]" (Hebrews 6:12).

Remember that Laziness and disorganization can be exploited by the devil to ruin your respect and affection for one another and, thus, harm your marriage. Modest clothes and clean, well-groomed bodies are vital for both husband and wife. Both couples should take care to create a home environment that is clean and organized, as this will promote serenity and calmness.

A lazy, shiftless husband who does not contribute to the household is a disadvantage to the family and is displeasing to God. Everything done for one another should be done with care and respect. Carelessness in these seemingly trivial concerns has caused discord in countless homes.

Insight:

Until marriage is founded on Christ Jesus being the Rock, the foundation of such a relationship or marriage is shakeable. God is the originator of marriage, therefore He should be consulted and He should be the rock that holds it.

If you can key into these biblical keys, our home, the relationship shall be bliss on earth.